I0560162

Soul DATES

EDWIN TORRES

This book is written to provide information and motivation to readers. Its purpose is not to render any type of psychological, legal, or professional advice of any kind. The content is the sole opinion and expression of the author, and not necessarily that of the publisher.

Copyright © 2023 by Edwin Torres.

All rights reserved. No part of this book may be reproduced, transmitted, or distributed in any form by any means, including, but not limited to, recording, photocopying, or taking screenshots of parts of the book, without prior written permission from the author or the publisher. Brief quotations for noncommercial purposes, such as book reviews, permitted by Fair Use of the U.S. Copyright Law, are allowed without written permissions, as long as such quotations do not cause damage to the book's commercial value. For permissions, write to the publisher, whose address is stated below.

Printed in the United States of America.

ISBN   978-1-955363-88-4   (Paperback)
ISBN   978-1-955363-89-1   (Digital)

Lettra Press books may be ordered through booksellers or by contacting:

Lettra Press LLC
30 N Gould St. Suite 4753
Sheridan, WY 82801
1 307-200-3414 | info@lettrapress.com
www.lettrapress.com

Table of Contents

All Love 1

Anthology of Love 3

Anointed Heart 6

Around the Globe 8

Because of You 10

B.E.S.T. (Better Everytime Staying True) 11

Body Of Love.. 13

Come to Me.. 15

Companion... 17

Debt for Love 19

Deity.. 21

Deity 2.. 23

Destined to Be... 24

Dream.. 26

Eternal Passion.. 28

Flourished Happiness 30

Forever 32

Forgiveness 34

Gentle Passion... 36

Genuine.. 38

G.I.R.L. (Girl I Really Love) 41

G.O.A.T. (Girl of All Traits)............................... 43

Going to You.. 45

Heavenly Love 46

Healing Passion...48

Heart...50

Heart And Soul 52

Hero..54

Inspirational 56

Internal Love...58

Journey...60

Letter to You 62

Like No Other..64

Love Intimate..66

Love Story...67

Nostalgia...69

One for Another 71

One Two Three Love 73

Out of this World 74

Pathway to Love..75

Priceless 77

Significant Other 79

Soul & Heart..81

Soul Dates...83

Sunshine..85

Unforgettable 87

Until the End..88

Vanity Closure 90

You and I...92

You Can Be Free...93

All Love

Come here sweety
Let's make a treaty.
For us to become a pair
So come and take my chair.
Baby girl you can sit
You're the reason
That my heart is lit
My love releasing
Every single bit
My heart you're teasing
Come for all of it
My love is not for leasing.
Because it's for you to own
Just baby for you alone
To you my hearts have flown
Baby let me hear your tone.
Right after the first ring
With all the love you bring
Go on girl do your thing
I'll give you my heart with a sling.
So you can have it strapped
Or maybe have it wrapped
The wings in my heart flapped
I kissed you and I got slapped.

But it was worth the risk
Baby I'm the one you frisk.
You're padding me down
Just don't be mad at me now
Because it's all love.

Anthology of Love

I'll love you to the moon
Stand by my side
When nights are gloom
Baby come on let's hide
Happy times will loom
My love came from a tide
Let me be your groom
So you can be my bride
All the way until my doom
Now you no longer cried
See all our love bloom
Always from the inside.
You make me wonder
Would you take my heart
And everything under
When my love's in a chart
You'll get a high number
Baby I'll go to the mart
If you're afraid of thunder.
I want you to feel
Every day protected
Have your heart sealed
After I connected.
Let my love enter her

In my empire
You're the emperor
Whenever she's tired.
Then carry her
If she's the one
Then marry her
Until life is done.
I'll give you an X-ray
To see the inner you
Read what your texts say
With the glimmer through
And then the next day
No longer dimmer too.
At any time of night
You shine so bright
You're so fine and right
My heart is in your line of sight.
Baby come take it
Love it but don't fake it
And please don't break it.
I'll re write this fairy tale
If you're in a scary jail
I won't even dare to fail
Just prepare your bail
You and I a pair prevails.
But you rescued me
With you my struggling ends
Being yours I'm blessed to be
More than a couple of friends.
We'll be partners
When things get harder.

Baby you make it smooth
Your heart I want to soothe
Take you back to your youth
With every word from my tooth.
None of it is dental
From the heart it's cardio
Some of it is mental
How happy are we though.
Baby your face
I want to caress
And then replace
All of your stress
You're heart I'll trace
What I want to possess
Let's start the race
You got me obsessed.
So baby come to me.

Anointed Heart

If My Heart Was a City
You would be the mayor
In this game of love
There's only two players
When the days are grayer.
Your light is fluorescent
What I would do for your scent
Baby I'll become your peasant
Your body has shapes of crescents
Inside your heart I am present.
And I plan to stay all the way.
Baby just stay patient
You and I take a vacation.
In a place just to relax
My love for you is at its max
And on that I'll never lax
If I have to I'll even pay a tax
I'll rub your skin with some wax.
Now you're feeling sticky
Just a little bit icky
Please honey don't be picky.
To your side I'll go quickly
My love is only for you strictly
Without you my heart becomes sickly.

Baby you are my medication
For your love is my dedication
All the others went to religation
I love you with no hesitation
I'll be glad to give a demonstration
But maybe after my meditation.
For your love my heart strains
But it's okay baby I feel no pain
Instead I feel your love through my veins
It's very clear and plain
I'll leave your heart with my stain.
Baby girl now your heart is anointed
It's to your soul I'm appointed
I promise baby you won't be disappointed.
Because I'm here to make you happy.

Around the Globe

My Love for You
Is something across the nation
Or maybe worldwide
I want to show my appreciation
For being by my side.
You're the one I care for
My love for you is airborne
Maybe you and I can share more
Girls like you are a rare form.
With your heart I'm missing in there
To conquer it I'm mission prepared
But in reality your soul isn't that scared
I come to you when I'm vision impaired.
So you can be my opticals
I'll write our love chronicles
We laugh at something comical.
Baby with you it feels like magic
Something very nostalgic
Without you it's tragic
So I start to just panic.
If you're feeling blessed
Baby let's go for the prize
Honey if you're a mess
You're the one I organize.

It's your heart I reconstruct
With all the love we conduct
Because since the day of your birth
They couldn't pay what your worth
Don't worry baby I say you're my earth.
Around the globe.

Because of You

I want to make you my spouse
Give you a house
But I can only afford
To buy you a blouse.
Even though you deserve more
These days my love you reserved for.
Your face I want to caress
And your love to regress
Without you there could be less
That's the reason I obsess
Because I just want us to progress
I just want all our success.
So we can proceed
To love with no need
And we can go lead.
Be an example for couples
Baby with you
It's my love that I smuggle.
I love this feeling
Because I know it's the real thing
That has me going through the ceiling.
All the way up in a cloud
No cheating allowed.
Baby you're like the birds in the morning
How wonderful my day is forming.
Because of you.

B.E.S.T. (Better Everytime Staying True)

Baby You Are
The best part of me
I feel your love
Pass through my arteries.
I move to you with haste
To put my hands on your waist
And your lips to taste
To stick to you like paste.
You're a wonderful spectacle
So about us don't feel skeptical.
Us together it might be
Something to enjoy nightly
To hold you so tightly
And love you so rightly
Taking things lightly
The only one my sight sees.
You should be on a billboard
The one my heart is filled for
Baby I love you still more.
As a matter of fact

I love you the most
From coast to coast
You and me intact
In my heart you're the host.
The head of the show
Carry you to bed when we go
Love me you said it I know.
I want to whisper in your ear
Tell me baby is it really clear
Only thing missing is me dear.
Of you my heart is full
So you're the one I pull
Myself towards
And I move forward.
Without you I tend to move
Always way back
But you always prove
Other girls stay whack.
Because you're the best.

Body Of Love

I got you in my heart
I hope that's where you got me
You can have any part of my body
My lips and my tongue
My liver my lungs.
Take away my brain
If it'll fade away your pain
I love your hips and thighs
Your lips and eyes.
You're more precious
Than a gold treasure
Who takes away
My whole pressure
With your heart, mind, body, and soul
I enjoy those pleasures.
Let me shower you
With nothing but love and affection
So baby make me your selection
Because you define perfection
You have no need to make corrections
Look in my eyes and see your reflection
Come baby let's make a connection
So I can be

Your truest guy
Let it be you and I
Who knew the lie
When we flew so high.

Come to Me

Baby
You're in my soul
When you're not there
It's just a big hole
So I start to get scared.
From the thought of losing you
It's not something I'll be choosing to
On your feet your shoes are new.
You and I made a deal
To always stay real.
Our love none is hype
Only the real type
Blow you a kiss through a pipe
Honey you're my stars and stripes
Baby please don't ever gripe.
You fill my stomach
When it grumbles
That's why I remain humble
Let me hear you mumble
Thanks to you I never stumble.
In your path I walk straight
It's due to all of your traits
Which no one can debate.
Girl come love me please

For you my heart skips a beat
Watch my sadness decrease
When I'm concerned I ask did you eat
I'm the one that you tease
When we're in the bed or the seat
See my happiness increase
And I love the way you're so neat.
If you walk in front
I'll follow behind
Our love isn't blunt
Honey let's rewind
Without you I grunt
And I can be blind.
Our love will never stunt.
A true love that we find.
So baby come to me.

Companion

Baby it's your heart
I want to steal and keep
Because it's really deep
Bad dreams heal with sleep
Take what I feel in heaps.
Tell me your frustrations
You and I only in us nation.
Let me love you
Baby allow me
Let the world know
I feel very proudly
You're my girl so
I say it very loudly.
Do you think I can have a chance
Maybe after just one dance
Or after we give each other a glance
To you my heart will prance.
It's a feeling
I never felt before
That has me
Feeling well for sure
Give me your hand
And I'll tell you more
I'm not a doctor

Trying to sell you cures.
I'm the one
Who came to heal you
Because I feel
What you feel too
It's so very real
That it's sealed through.
You're the reason I shine
Inside I'm beaming
You're truly the divine
No I'm not dreaming
Just look at the signs
And say the meaning.
I want this to never end
Because you're a goddess
That was heaven sent.

Debt for Love

As I sit here
I might start to think
I'll give you my heart in pink.
Baby come explore my mind
Because you're more than kind
Everything is yours to find
You either see it or you're blind.
Baby you've got me feeling funny ways
Because you're more beautiful
Than a sunny day.
You give my stomach little butterflies
So I dedicate to you this lullaby
Now maybe you can love a guy
Through your path I'm cutting by
To see you just stay put and I.
May come to your window
Just let me in though.
I'll give your finger a little circle
On top there's a diamond
That is covered in purple
You and I on an island
As we're jumping through hurdles.
Every day my heart beats hard
Only for you sweetheart.

My love for you
Is like the national debt
It rises daily by the trillions
That's the way it was set
And it's for life.

Deity

What do I do
With these thoughts
Delightful feelings
That you've brought.
Only thing I can do is dream
That I'm the one that found you
I want to make you my queen
So please let me crown you
When you're the one I've seen
Then I get nervous around you
If you don't know what I mean
All my love will drowned you.
You're inside of my mind
And I refuse to forget
When you're the one I can't find
My heart gets upset
If I can't see you I'm blind
It's what I mostly regret.
In every other woman
I see your face
And your name I see
In every other place.
You're the cure to my virus
Without you my life is in crisis

If I become your osiris
Then will you be my Isis.
So when I call you a Goddess
I'm not being modest
I'm just being honest
And baby I promise.
Sorry I can't help what I feel
But I can only tell you it's real
In this everything I felt is revealed
The words I want to yell are concealed
Waiting for the day you open them
So I'm just here hoping when.

Deity 2

That time will come
For you to say that I'm the one
You might already have someone
So I leave you this note
Without you my mission is undone
These are more than just quotes
My heart is where this comes from
Every word that I wrote.
I hope you don't think it's weird
Please don't be scared
If I can't have you here
Then I want to be there
To whisper in your ear
How much that I care.
Perhaps I might be doing wrong
But these feelings that grew along
Are deep and too too strong.
You can have my soul to keep
Without you it's just a hole too deep
I think of you before I go to sleep.
Just know I'm your prince charming
If it's your soul he's been harming.
So much I want to be with you
And forever see it through.
For you I refuse to surrender.

Destined to Be

Baby
Tell me where you are
I want to take
Never share your heart
Every time I see you
I stare at art
Your soul
I will never tare apart
Or tell me how
Because I care to start
You turn my eyes
Into a pair of stars.
Come and have the best of me
Yes love it's our destiny
The one I request to see
So now it's a quest to be
And maybe you guess that we
Could never date
Or can't relate
You have an appointment with my heart
Don't be late.
Why don't you come with me
On this journey
With all your passion

That burns me.
I offer you all my love
I'd give you the world
But it's not enough
You're as pretty as a dove
Who has me handcuffed
No girl is on your level
You are above.
The queen of my kingdom
With your feelings just bring some
Your castle the bells ring from.
Inside this temple
You're a goddess.

Dream

Life isn't always how it seems
Should've known when I met you
You would be the girl of my dreams
Should've treated you like a queen
But I chose to let you go
So I could roll with the fiends
And if at times I acted really mean
Just know I'm not the type to sex you
And then leave the scene
Baby if you cook then I'll clean.
We can share the household chores
As long as you have desire
Of making me yours
I love being a gentleman
Opening doors.
For you to go through
But you prefer going to spots
Where people don't know you.
Because of you
My heart is very large
In there you are in charge.
In my heart build your home
If in yours you're still alone
My soul when will you own.

Because you got me possessed
Our relationship is the best
With you no girl could contest
Without you my heart is in unrest.
Come fill my loneliness
If I don't know about love
Then baby show me this
Each other we know we miss.
Every night I dream of you
And hug the pillow
I'm alone still though
My heart you fill so
Your tears will spill no
Like leaves from a willow
Now you and I will know
They'll never touch the floor.

Eternal Passion

You had left
Now back in my heart you're welcome
Because their acts of love were seldom
Your heart and soul I held them
Now your beauty melts men.
Why are you so gorgeous
Like the Sun God Horus
In my mind you're the chorus
I hear what you repeat for us.
When you were cold and shook
Where were you told to look
In your arms you hold your crook.
Because it's your heart I rob
Baby loving you is my job
My heart has a door turn the knob.
Honey you don't need a key
The door isn't locked
Let your love exceed with me
It can never be blocked
I'll move to you speedily
Too fast to be clocked.
You're the one I want to grab
So you're the one I'm pulling by
To make a lot of you in a lab

Then your love to multiply
When we go out I got the tab
From your love I'm full and high.
To you I have an extension
Only to connect in another dimension
Where our love can retire with a pension.
And we can live to the end.

Flourished Happiness

In Our Hearts
We saw growth
What we have now
Is the fruit of our oath
We made a vow
That we honor both.
Honey with you
Everything is possible
But without you
Everything is horrible.
I love coming home
To a warm meal
Now it is known
You were born real.
Talk to me and I'll listen
It's your head that I'm kissing
I see your heart always glisten
I will always love this thing.
So baby when you're feeling ill
You can just lay back and chill
I will clean up all the spills
When you wake up I'm cleaning still
Let me love you with all my will
So you and I can have a thrill.

All of your love is my bill
And I'm your sleeping pill
Out the window sill.
You always look
As you cook
I'll write you a book
It's my heart that you took.
We can just lay and rest
If your day is stressed
Think it's good to stay in best
Games we're playing less.
For you my heart was built
Let me hold you under a quilt
Baby never feel guilt
How much of your tears spilt
Now it's tears of happiness.

Forever

You're the one
I want to love every minute
So I give myself a limit
To open your heart and be in it
And my heart gets a tingly feeling
For all the things I'm revealing.
So now baby no more shedding tears
Because now I'm spreading cheers
You and I moving ahead in here.
If you're the one I meet
I'll show you gratitude
You're the one I greet
I won't give you attitude
I'll give you my seat
And address your attributes.
Baby don't ever stop all your charm
Why don't you drop in my arms
I'm going to chop all your harm
You're the crop in my farm.
Now I make you a shrine
You're the one I deserve
I love all your lines
And all of your curves
Our love at it's prime

It's what I preserve.
You're the one I address to
With the greatest passion
I just want to dress you
In the latest fashion.
And then some more
Baby don't feel unsure
You're the one I'll come for
To walk through one door
That will close forever.

Forgiveness

Yes I can tell you're the nicest
Men don't know your worth
Because you are priceless.
I tell you this as a friend
It's not about sex to all men.
Now I know how you feel
Something to heal
So many times attempted
But was unaccepted
The things in life reflected
A love no man respected
Maybe in a new year
Everything is perfected
After the mistakes corrected.
So I just want to wish you the best
And dismiss all your stress
Get a man
To be kissed and caressed
If you're feeling dissed and depressed
Looking for your medication
This is it yes
Real love does exist you could guess.
Hope you truly find your happiness.
If you're not here

You are badly missed
The one I would gladly kiss
90% of the guys weren't good enough
Some of them couldn't love.
But you still stood it tough.
Focus on only you
Don't worry at nights
I get lonely too
Don't mess with these phony dudes.
Those who know you
Gave your soul to
And wouldn't hold
you Or console you
Were after something else
When they rolled through.
Well I hope this can cheer you up
I'm glad you say hi
Whenever you walk through
I'll be there
Should you need someone to talk to.

Gentle Passion

If I'm the one
You antagonize
Sweety I apologize
Then I start to agonize.
Baby I'm your temple
Inside your worshipped
I start to tremble
If your heart slipped
What does it resemble
A heart that was nipped.
But I did it gently
Just something friendly.
Without you I feel cursed
Something real worse
I'll give you a steel purse.
Because it's that heavy
But your heart has a levy.
Your love imposed
After it was enclosed.
Inside I'm barracated
Our love activated
Feels very animated
Your heart is laminated.
Gotta keep it protected

Baby I'm your armor
When bad is detected
Don't let anyone harm her.
Become her shield
In the battlefield
But don't ever yield.
Just never give up.

Genuine

Baby it's okay
I think of you
The whole day.
You went and came back
Because others had the same act
Words that are game packed.
Not one of those guys
Trying to get in your pants
Lie to you I can't
Hear all the love that I chant.
You got me provoked
After my heart was broke
My soul you awoke
Everytime that you spoke
You're the weed that I smoke.
That has me high
Baby just ask me why
As you're passing by.
When your soul I get
Then my goal is set
If you're cold and wet.
Baby I'll dry you
And warm you
Maybe if I try to

I can reform too.
You're more than the one I want
You're the one I need
With you I always flaunt
But most importantly I succeed.
Baby my heart
Is yours to discover
Your man is here
Come be his lover.
Love how it is to be
You should be kissing me
So we can make history.
Something to remember
And always be tender
A goddess they send her.
To shine the light
When the time is right.
We're lovers currently
Without one another
We were miserable weren't we.
So if I give you a house
Will you give me a home
If I give you a crown
Will you give me a throne
When I come around
Do not leave me alone
If I'm feeling down
Will you come in my zone
If you could be found
So I can make you my own
When I move to your town

It's cuz my love has just grown.
Now it's immense
Best part
Is that it's intense
In my heart
It makes sense
Don't depart
Or dispense
You're a form of art.
That can't be drawn
Baby let's kiss
Until the break of dawn
Then awake and yawn.
And be the first face I see
In every single place I be
You're name stays with me
In my heart it's embedded.

G.I.R.L.
(Girl I Really Love)

When You're in My Mind
Then I get very pensive
I see you even being blind
My love for you is extensive.
To win your heart I'm determined
Because inside the desire is burning.
Just going really wild
Then your number I dialed
For your heart I filed.
Only so I can fill it
Baby I can will it
So let me fulfill it.
My heart to you submitted
After an act of love committed.
Best part we're both guilty
Inside your love has filled me.
But inside it's too much
So with you I share
My soul you've touched
Just be aware.
You're the one I want to hug
Because you're so cuddly

We can lay and kiss on the rug
And do it utterly.
I will always treat you with dignity
And love you until infinity
Baby please don't limit me
My heart is your vicinity.
Baby there's no denial
I like your style
I think of you all while
Take my love in piles
Because it extends for miles
Feel it in the isle
Or drink it from a vial.
Your love is my controlled substance
That I want to have in abundance.

G.O.A.T.
(Girl of All Traits)

Girl If You're Feeling Hurt
Then join me on this trip
Put on a pretty skirt
But one that won't rip
I'll wear your favorite shirt
If you let me kiss your lips
These words I blurt
Won't let your heart drip
If you're feeling like dirt
I'll hold you with a tight grip.
Whenever you're sad
Let me hear your pleas
My love you always had
All over the seven seas.
That for you I'll sail
To be together
Travel through hail
Or any weather
I'll read the mail
You write with a feather.
Baby with you I have wings
I feel like I can fly

At any time in the spring
In a beautiful sky
I'm attached to your string
Baby tell me why
Just hear my love ring
Everytime that you cry
Be my lifelong fling
When you're passing by.
My love get in the car
I'll give you a ride
If you're somewhere far
I would've flied
Tell me where you are
I'll go to your side
Now you got new scars
When all of them lied.
If you want truth
Baby with you I float
Word from my tooth
Is that you're the GOAT
That's Greatest Of All Time.

Going to You

If Your Love is a Ship
Then my heart is your port
Look how tall it came
If my love was a sport
You'd make the hall of fame
A feeling of some sort
Don't let it stall the game.
My heart is on love mode
We speak with a love code
You're gonna make me explode
I love you by the loads
Baby you and I hit the road.
Now we're on a voyage
And everything is joyous
I won't ever destroy this
Let me be your boy miss.
Where we'll meet
I'll show up early there
A love we'll surely share
I love all your curly hair
And all your girly wear
You and I a pearly pair
Our love in the swirly air
Because it's not seen but felt.

Heavenly Love

You're the Energy
That enters me
Keeps me balanced
And centers me.
With you everything is heavenly
So I will love you endlessly.
In every emergency
Because it's my tendency.
Always a friend to me
Never a pretend to be
So I give thanks
For the goddess sent to me
To bless me
From Earth to the heavens
I've been calling for
your love
When you fall
You are falling in my glove
You're my princess queen and goddess
And all of the above.
I'll love you for the rest of my life
Or it's done
I want you
For more than fun

A true love
That sure will come
I'm not ashamed baby
To say you're the one.
If you're crying for love
Or lack there of
Just know that I care love
So we can share stuff.

Healing Passion

Let me paint you a world
That's full of colors
But first let's be lovers
I see you and think of my mother
Two women like no other.
Baby I give you thanks
Let's start a sheet in blank
For you I'll walk the plank
Your love I just drank
My soul you can crank
Baby it isn't a prank
I'm the one that you yank
And my heart is your bank.
Because my love you deposit
Don't worry baby I haven't lost it.
But can I pay the interest
Tell me my princess
Without you I'm winless.
So the moral of this story
Is that you are my glory
What I want for me
Is for you to adore me.
Is the feeling mutual
Or the same as usual.

From my eyes the tears drop
When will the fear stop
But baby I'm your clear top.
Now you are there suffering
While the lonely guy no one's loving him.
Baby in this game of chess
You are the queen
But I will aim and press
Whatever button I've seen
Baby you came the best
Like nature in green.
Because you're that pure
You're the one I lure
To get me the cure.
Now I'm healed.

Heart

Honey
You're the one I'm missing
But I manage to stand tough
Put me in your love prison
But don't keep me handcuffed
You and I have risen
You are all of this man's stuff.
If you see my words repeat
It's because there's not enough to explain
With you I'll never see defeat
You are the one that I gain
My most memorable feat
Is when I can take away your pain
If you and I don't meet
Then I'm always going insane
You're the trick to my treat
It's all my love that you drain.
You and I are a perfect match
So let all of our love hatch
But it will never detach
Because it's secured with a latch
Now give me your love batch
It's your heart that I snatch
If it needs to be patched.

That means your heart just broke
I love you baby and It's not a joke
Until the day when I croak.
Then your love will resurrect me
Your heart will do the rest correctly.
Because like the Legend Of Zelda
Every little piece of your heart
Gives me life.

Heart And Soul

Baby you shine
Too bright
With every new line
You write.
Now a new love is written
With gloves and mittens.
Because your hands are warm
Without you
I'm hurt and I'm torn
Your heart is the land I form.
So I will cultivate it
My heart
So full you made it..
Without you I feel empty
Tell your heart to tempt me
To the end of the world it sent me.
From there I await
To begin our fate
My heart is your bait
Come and open the gate.
My love is your courtyard
Because it's full of flowers
Baby I give you four stars
There's no love like ours

We can meet at a sports bar
For a couple of hours.
Have a piece of my cake
While the candles spark
Or we can take
A walk in the park
And we can awake
Alone in the dark
Let's kiss by the lake
In the car when I'm parked
It's your heart that I make
A new trip to embark
Make no mistake
I'm leaving my mark
In your heart and soul.

Hero

From my heart
You never departed
From the beginning
When it started
With you I am winning
I become warm hearted
It's no more sinning.
Have a child
And go to work
I always smile
Because you're the perks
Baby I love your style
Promise not to be a jerk
At times when I'm wild
You give me a smirk.
Girl don't be upset
The sun is not up yet.
I love everything
That you bring
And when you sing
Baby let's have a swing.
When we look eye to eye
You and I flying high.
Then see the horizon

And the sun rising
With your uprising
But not surprising.
Because you're my hero.

Inspirational

You're the one
I want to squeeze
But I see you and I freeze.
Like I just got cold
Let the page unfold
Baby you've become bold.
I love all of your features
With you no other compares
Being without you is unfair.
You're the one I'll fight for
All the way to the end
You inspire me to write more
So I just pick up a pen
Do you want to take a flight or
Just let me know when.
Now baby forgive me if I'm wrong
For coming off too high strong
I want to be with you all night long
Sing and dance to love songs.
When you're not here
Then I start to yearn
I see it very clear
A lesson I learn
Is to have no fear

Because you will return.
It's my heart you filled
When I was almost killed.
From a heart broken
It can only be healed
When inside you it's soaken
To have everything revealed.
With a magic lamp
Honey your hair is damp
My love for you I cramp.
Because there's no more space
So we go to a different place.
Where our love can spread.

Internal Love

If you're heart is broken
Then it's mine you borrow
If you're feeling hurt today
I'll heal you tomorrow
Trying to find a new way
To get rid of your sorrows
I'll listen to what you say.
It's my heart you follow
So full of you it can't be hollow.
With you I treat everything passively
Because I love you massively.
More than the height
Of a skyscraper
These feelings I write
Are on my paper.
Now I'll sign the contract
For our hearts to make contact
In a place where it's compact.
In our love we drowned
Nowhere to be found
You're the one I crowned
Everytime I came around
Because you're world renowned.
With both my feet on the ground.

You're the reason I'm standing
In your heart my love is landing
Inside mines you're commanding.
My commander and chief
I ask myself is it her
Tell me will it be brief
Am I just a visitor
When I'm going through grief
How can this occur.
When you're not here I'm dying
When you're here I'm flying
So it's on you I'm spying
If you're ever sad I'm crying
Because inside my heart is frying.
Every time it burns
With the blood it pumps
This time it's the turn
Of your heart to jump.
Into my soul.

Journey

Let me be your wish
Tell me your feelings
In this sea of fish
You're the one I reel in
I'll prepare your dish
And your heart I'm stealing.
I'll be your genie
From a magic lamp
You haven't seen me
It's my heart you stamp
Love me so meanly
So I can be your champ
Everything is teeny
In your heart I camp.
It's just us and the elements
To make our love so relevant
Because your feelings I fell in them.
Girl you got me trapped
With my hands strapped
But for you I clapped
You and I just napped.
Goddess I ask you for a prayer
Because you're higher than the pope
Baby it's okay don't be scared

If you're feeling no hope
Tell me if you are so aware
That my heart has just broke
Now I'm going through despair
So I tell you in this note
Just know that I care
Because with you I gloat
Your whole body is my lair
You understand my quotes
At you I look and I stare
It's your heart that I grope
Baby don't ever dare
To detach from my rope
Tell my babe what to wear
When we're hitting the slopes
See your dress with a tair
Whenever we elope
Now everything is fair
Very cool and it's dope.
To have your love.

Letter to You

I may not be your first
But I want to be your last
Without you I'm cursed
It's a spell that you cast.
Because you got me hypnotized
I'll take a look in both eyes
Leaving you is not wise.
Love the way your so witty
Let's spend our day in the city
Baby you're as cute as a kitty
With you I never feel pity.
I will make you happy
When you're feeling down
If your day is crappy
I'll eliminate your frown
And make it snappy
Put on your gown.
In my heart you graduated
So congratulations
I'm very glad you made it
Know on graduations.
From my heart it's a tradition
To love you under any condition
You're the cause of my ambition.

Sweety you're my jewel
My heart is yours to rule
I see you and start to drool
Because without you I'm a fool
With you everything is cool
Baby take a seat on the stool.
I have a surprise
Just sit and think
As I look in her eyes
Smile and wink
Or give me a sign.

Like No Other

You're more than royalty
Because you are holy
For only you is my loyalty
I remember what you told me.
Baby you're the star of my movie
Because everything with you is groovy
Inside honey you move me
And baby you proved we.
Can be a unit
Didn't think
That we can do it
Hear us clink.
Through the sound we gave
If you see me around then wave
I'm the one you found and saved.
I want to return the favor
So just tell me darling
And I'll begin the labor
Even if it's a hard thing.
I'll give you my sweat and tears
And ask myself how did you get in here
Now everything is set and clear
Every day I'm glad we met my dear
Don't drive your heart just let it steer.

And see where it takes you
What won't break you
Will make you
I will never forsake you.
In every other girl's face
You're the one I'm seeing
Baby I love your grace
And all of your being.
When you weren't here I cried
Because I'm the one you denied
I said I love you and never lied
You got to admit at least I tried.
Let me do it again.

Love Intimate

With you
All the good has begun
I'm so glad that I found you
You're my sky and sun
My world revolves around you.
Baby let's get intimate
Because my love for you is infinite.
Let's have a hug and rejoice
You're the drug of my choice
And I am loving your voice.
So don't ever stop speaking
You got everything I'm seeking
Close your eyes sweetie no peeking.
Don't know what I should propose
With every single line I compose
My love tell me what you suppose
Just as long as you're not opposed.
If it's your heart I conquer
Then it's your love I honor.
Until that time has come
Believe that I'm the one
Baby you shine my sun.

Love Story

Thank you
For wanting to be with me
And everything you see in me
You'll always be my deity.
So I call you the divine
Because you're more fine
Than a bottle of old wine
Just thankful that you're mine.
Truly love me
You're the one to do it first
When I've been through it worst.
My heart is yours for the taking.
Watch phony guys
There's more of them faking
I'll fix your heart
When it's torn or it is breaking.
Put it together and keep it forever
Though we're not sleeping together
Because the feeling is deeper whenever.
So far inside
But hard to hide
Let's start the ride
And let our hearts collide
For you I'll wear my scars with pride.

I want to hold you close
And give you a stolen rose
Because it's my soul you chose
You can have my heart
By the whole or dosed.
Baby I'm here to cuddle
Come in my arms
Tell me your fears and troubles
I want to whisper in your ear and snuggle
Glasses of champagne
Say cheers with bubbles.
You're the reason I'm up so late
Thinking of my soul mate
But I'm the one you won't date
So much love with you
I'll feel no hate
Let's live a love story.

Nostalgia

I appreciate
All your love I receive
It's an essential sensation
With you I believe
In sentimental relations
But I tend to grieve
When detrimental is patience.
Because your way
I tend to step
So I press replay
Go back when you slept
The message I relay
Is the secret your friends have kept.
What you've concealed
Is actually unreal.
It's too good to be true
How could it be you
I should be it too.
I'm still waiting
For your man to be
It's my deepest fantasy
So just give your hand to me.
So we can touch our palms
Your hands will be my balm

I rub my skin and I'm calm.
Because you're the one I'm into
So I write this trying to win you
Baby tell me what you've been through
Your previous love forget him boo.
Let me be your ghost
Just like Casper
So we can get close
Just a little faster
I love you the most
In my heart you're the master
Why don't we make a toast
Without you I'm a disaster.
Let our body skins rub
My heart is your hub
My body is your tub
The inside you scrub.
Because with you I'm clean.

One for Another

Without You I Feel Lost
Help me find the way
In my heart you're the boss
At any single time of day.
You're the one I want to elevate
So baby you and I can celebrate
If you love me then yell it mate
Because baby I know you well to date
In love with you I fell at eight
Because of you I can tell it's great
My heart isn't for selling rates.
It's with all your love I'm paid
Baby in me all your love is made
In my book you have an A grade
So baby let's go to the everglades
You're the one I want to serenade.
Without you my heart is frozen
You can melt the ice
If I'm the one you've chosen
Then baby yell it twice
My love you're exposing
Having your help is nice
Everytime I see you posing.
For the camera say cheese

But games don't play please
Without you I'm every day ceased
With you I always stay eased.
I'll become you're love slave
For all the love you gave
When you're situation is grave
That's when I become brave
But I promise I won't misbehave.

One Two Three Love

Let's kiss
Under the mistletoe
While we hear
The whistle blow
Now it's clear.
Like the water
That quenches my thirst
Love you is what I will do first.
And love you I will do second
After you get my salutation
It's your heart and soul I reckoned
After careful calculation.
And I will love you third
With every single word
My heart beat you heard.
And last but not least
With you I finally got peace.
Baby you're the best
I got you in my chest
Everytime I hit the nest
Just to lay my head and rest
You appear in my dreams.

Out of this World

Love me
You're the one to do it first
What I feel for you
Is larger than the universe
What I reveal is new
Without you I go to a hearse
What is concealed is true.
It's your heart
I want to explore with a probe
Baby you're smart
And the prettiest in the globe.
If my girl you are
Never see me stress
If you're somewhere far
I'll locate you without GPS.
You're my friend and my girl
Let's go to the end of the world.
Baby come keep me company
And see what you've done to me
Because my love comes for free.
The best things in life
Can't be paid
I can't wait until my wife
You are made.

Pathway to Love

Get to know her
See her personality
Take out her insanity
What's your nationality.
Speak to me in a language foreign
If you already have love let more in.
So take yours and mine
Let them combine
Just lay back and unwind
Like you there's only one kind.
Every night in my dream
You are super supreme
Eating cookies and cream
Hear your heart when it screams.
Baby tell me what you've felt
Just played the cards you were delt
Pulled your pants up without a belt.
Everytime you always fell
Straight down into hell
But no one heard you yell
And you turned out very well
In your heart I want to dwell
Baby you have a story to tell
Of when you were trapped in a cell.

Then you escaped
And your knee got scraped.
So I carried you on my back
Baby I got what you lack
Heart and soul the whole pack
It was hard when you sold snacks
My heart is shattered don't let it crack
Your heart and mine on the same track.
On the pathway to love.

Priceless

Baby you're my stars and moon
You can have my heart and wound
Because you and I aren't doomed.
It really feels
Like everything about you is to close
I just want to go and kiss your nose.
A damaged heart
Now has her wishing
Someone would conquer it
With her permission.
You're the one I want to hold
Because your heart and soul
Are a million times
More precious than gold
Yes you have now been told
Let's make this last and grow old
My soul is yours it wasn't sold
I feel all your warmness when
I'm cold. In the weather of any form
Baby I am keeping you warm.
So sweetheart run to me
Right now my love
You have some to see
Let's find out

What this comes to be
Maybe the root
That came from a tree.
Because it will be
Strong and rise
The others had you living
The longest lies In reality baby
Those were the wrongest guys
Let me wipe those tears
Along your eyes
What do you respond
When I say we bond
So baby let's be fond.
Of one another
On you my love I'll smother.

Significant Other

In this Love Story
You're the star of the cast
I'll erase all of your past
Because my love is vast
If it's us you grasp
Then baby just ask.
You're the one I clutch
After your heart I touch
Because I love you very much
A girl like you there's none such.
I'll give up watching the game on T.V.
So you can watch your program
Now baby let's hold hands
And slow dance
To some old jams
Of romance
You make me feel like no man.
Baby I can't stand the fights
Let's have all our issues handled right
So on any random night
We can make love under the candle lights.
Then you and I cuddle
My love is in a puddle
Under some rubble

I send you heart bubbles
But you got me muddled.
Honey you're so loveable
Like a teddy bear so huggable
Just please don't be gullible.
Okay my significant other.

Soul & Heart

The idea of us you ponder
If it's your heart I conquer
Baby then let's be fonder.
As I type this on the keyboard
You're the one I want to be for
So now it's to your love I resort
And it's to your heart I report.
Because our love is at its prime
So I'm here writing these lines
To you I'm composing a rhyme
It's your love that I won't resign
Us together is something made by design
Let your heart and my heart align.
Like the stars in the constellations
Baby let me just calm your patience.
If your feeling anxiety
Have my love
In all varieties
But baby don't lie to me
Because yours I'll die to be.
Whenever I kiss your lips
Then I'll start doing flips
Touch your heart at the tip
Watching all of my love drip

And now making a strip.
Your heart and soul each
Are what I desire to reach
Now I'm your love sucking leech
While you're eating a peach.
Enjoy it baby.

Soul Dates

You come first and second
Then maybe me
Come on baby be.
My love all the time
Like Bonnie and Clyde
We'll commit some crimes
It's you by my side
Then I'll make you mines
By your rules I'll abide
Just line by line
Baby don't let anything slide.
Loving you is pivotal
So I become meticulous
You say it's not that critical
Honey don't be ridiculous
I'll even perform a miracle
My heart is your stimulus.
I'll show you off
In every single coast
With your skin soft
You're the reason I boast.
I just gloat and I brag
Both In a row
You have my heart in a bag

Tied with a bow.
Everyday would be valentines day
If things would happen my way.
You're the one I want to uplift
Because you are my gift
With your heart I'll be swift
Feel all my love drift
Baby because to you it shifts.
Just like Link it's your heart I raise
Because you're the one I praise.
Now let's love one another.

Sunshine

Babe
I would never hurt you
Because I love your virtue.
Your heart and soul collected
After I'm the one you selected.
Now inside your heart
I'm the king
To rule every single part
Doing my thing.
I'll swallow my pride
Because you're a delight
Were your eyes dried
The tears clogged your sight
Baby even I cried
Let's never again fight.
I'll approach you
Just a little more subtle
So you and I can cuddle
Get wet in your puddle.
Girl keep me wet
You're the one I get
After the day we met
Our love has been set
Baby girl there's no regret.

If anything it's the opposite
Your heart I'm not dropping it
Our love nothing is stopping it.
Honey because it's too fast
And forever it will last
You can break my cast.
From both of my legs
Baby you are my pegs
In the morning I'm making you eggs.
Whenever it's sunny
Yes my honey
I'm filling your tummy
With something yummy
Because I love you.

Unforgettable

I bet they have regrets
For all the games
They must've played
It's you and I only
To trust and aid
I couldn't ask for a better girl
If I had you custom made.
These aren't words on sheet
They're feelings on paper I
promise her I won't cheat
The pain won't heal or escape her.
If you ask me maybe
Your my classy lady
So sassy baby.
So show me your emotions
You make me shiver
My love is your whole ocean
My heart is your river
I have all your love potions
Ask and I'll deliver
With love say your notions
Because I'm a giver.

Until the End

My love for you
Is always very abundant
But never very redundant.
I'll warm you
When you're feeling chilly
If you're jealous stop being silly.
You're the one I want to love
Put my hands on but never shove.
Sorry If i'm being rude
I ask your pardon
Please don't ever elude
You and I can bargain
You're the one I include
Building my garden.
Where you're the prettiest flower
In my heart you have the power
But with all my love you shower.
Come on baby don't be timid
All your love just give it
It's something very vivid
Girl your life just live it.
You make my heart illuminate
Everytime we communicate.
Baby you inspire me

You've got me entirely
Of me you write in your diary.
All the way until the end
Are you my girl or my friend
Either way your heart I mend
With all the love that I send.
It came from a root
Like the seed in a fruit
On our date I'm wearing a suit
And of joy I'm blowing the flute.
So follow the tune.

Vanity Closure

Let me feel
Your love enter me
In my heart it's an entity
That can reveal an identity.
If I'm the one you recognize
Then love just expect a prize
Our love is too big to select a size.
Something unimaginable
The way you dress is very fashionable
Inside your heart is just habitable.
That's where I want to reside
It will be just me you're beside
All the drama let's put it aside.
My heart is your palace
Where you drink from a chalice
Baby my intention is not malice.
And I love all your qualities
Be my leader
And I'll follow your policies
Honey I'm eager.
To give you a kiss
And live with my miss.
Grab her and hold her
When she needs some closure

Baby I'm your soldier
Here to give my heart exposure
Just so you can feel so sure.
If I ever leave
Where am I supposed to go
See me grieve
If it's not very close we grow
Got a trick up my sleeve
You're so pretty you even pose in shows.
To capture your beauty
On the screen
Baby you're the only cutey
On the scene
Loving you is my duty
Know what I mean.

You and I

You're so irresistible
Which is why everything is permissible
With our love so visible
And your lips so kissable.
Let's run our lips
And move our tongues
And listen to the words
You've just sung.
So I can go to your melody
Baby I promise to remain in fidelity.
I don't mind if it's monogamous
Or on the low keep it anonymous
But not something monotonous.
It could be you and I
Or I and you
Just look through my eyes
And I'm crying too.
Baby we share the pain
Which is why I care the same
At the end I want you to wear my name.
Do everything for her
And you'll keep moving forward
She'll be there whenever you're hurt.

You Can Be Free

If You're the Goddess
Let me be the lord
It's your love I implored
Come to me when you're bored
I'll buy you stuff I can't afford.
I love it when you call me handsome
You're my Galaxy just like Samsung
So let me hold you for ransom.
I'm the one you're heart is after
Until the day I am captured
Very gently grab her.
You're the one I'm addicted to
In the next life I'm picking you
So to you I stick like glue.
But you never knew
Now baby here is the clue
Our love just grew
Up to the sky so blue
With the birds that flew.
Give me your beak
You make my knees weak
Into your room I'll sneak
My love for you leaks.
Keep it contained

My heart you've obtained
Of you I never complained
You kept me dry when it rained.
Baby you can be my sun
After a light day
I know she's the one
When I might stay
Where will we flee for fun
You're my bright ray
Baby you want to see it done
Just the right way.
I'll paint you a rainbow
Don't let the pain show
Just remove your chain slow.
So baby girl you can be free.

www.ingramcontent.com/pod-product-compliance
Lightning Source LLC
Chambersburg PA
CBHW031222120626
46545CB00003B/951